THE ULTIMATE
10
Entertainment

Music Legends

By Mark Stewart

Gareth Stevens
Publishing

Please visit our web site at www.garethstevens.com.
For a free catalog describing Gareth Stevens Publishing's list of high-quality books, call 1-800-542-2595 (USA) or 1-800-387-3178 (Canada). Gareth Stevens Publishing's fax: 1-877-542-2596

Library of Congress Cataloging-in-Publication Data
Stewart, Mark, 1960–
   Music legends / by Mark Stewart.
       p. cm. — (The ultimate 10 : entertainment)
   Includes bibliographical references and index.
   ISBN-10: 0-8368-9165-1   ISBN-13: 978-0-8368-9165-2 (lib. bdg.)
   ISBN-10: 1-4339-2213-4   ISBN-13: 978-1-4339-2213-8 (soft cover)
   1. Musicians—Biography—Juvenile literature.2. Singers—Biography—Juvenile literature. 3. Rock
   groups—Juvenile literature. 4. Popular music—History and criticism—Juvenile literature. I. Title.
  ML3929.S74 2010
  782.42164092'2—dc22 [B]   2009008290

This edition first published in 2010 by
Gareth Stevens Publishing
A Weekly Reader® Company
1 Reader's Digest Road
Pleasantville, NY 10570-7000 USA

Copyright © 2010 by Gareth Stevens, Inc.

Executive Managing Editor: Lisa M. Herrington
Senior Designer: Keith Plechaty

Produced by Editorial Directions, Inc.

Art Direction and Page Production: The Design Lab

Picture credits
Key: t = top, b= bottom, c = center, l = left, r = right
Cover, title page: (t) Shutterstock, (c) Volker Hartmann/AFP/Getty Images, (bl) ©Underwood & Underwood/
CORBIS, (br) Michael Buckner/Getty Images for Thelonious Monk Institute; pp. 4–5, 35: ©Siggi Bucher/
Reuters/Corbis; p. 7: Bernard Gotfryd/Getty Images; p. 8: (t) John Pratt/Keystone/Getty Images, (b) ©Emilio
Lari/Rex Features/Courtesy Everett Collection; p. 9: ©Corbis; p. 11: ©Bettmann/Corbis; p. 12: (t) ©Michael
Ochs Archive/Corbis, (b) Henry Groskinksy/Time Life Pictures/Getty Images; p. 13: ©Everett Collection; p. 15:
Jan Persson/Redferns; p. 16: (t) ©20th Century Fox/Courtesy Everett Collection, (b) AP Photo/Dan Poush; p.
17: ©Jeff Christensen/Reuters/Corbis; p. 19: Aps/Sygma/Corbis; p. 20: (t) ©Michael Ochs Archives/Corbis,
(b) AP Photo /Xinhua, Chen Xiaowei; p. 21: ©Universal/Courtesy Everett Collection; p. 23: ©Bob Banner
Associates/Courtesy Everett Collection; p. 24: (t) ©Bettmann/Corbis, (b) ©Reuters/Corbis; p. 25: (t) Ke.Mazur/
WireImage, (b) ©Pat Benic/epa/Corbis; p. 27: Marc Sharrat/Rex Feartures/Courtesy Everett Collection; p. 28:
(t) ©Henry Kiltz/Corbis, (b) ©Adroach/Dreamstime.com; p. 29: ©Michael Ochs Archives/Getty Images; p.
31: (t) James Mitchell/Ebony Collection via AP Images, (b) ©Michael Ochs Archives/Corbis; p. 32: (t) ©Lynn
Goldsmith/Corbis, (b) ©MCA/Universal/Courtesy Everett Collection; p. 33: Kevin Mazur/WireImage; p. 36:
(t) ©Neal Preston/Corbis, (b) ©Jim Young/Reuters/Corbis; p. 37: ©Emmanuel Kwitema/Rcuters/Corbis; p.
39: ©Neal Preston/Corbis; p. 40: (t) Rex USA (157509D) Madonna in the video for "Like a Prayer"—1989
Courtesy Everett Collection, (b); p. 41: David Fisher/Rex USA/Courtesy Everett Collection; p. 43: PA Photo/
Mark Lennihan; p. 44: (t) Michael Ochs Archives/Getty Images, (b) James Devaney/WireImage; p. 45: KMazur/
WireImage; p. 46: (t) ©Henry Diltz/Corbis, (c) ©Denis O'Regan/Corbis, (b) ©Jeff Albertson/Corbis

Printed in the United States of America

1 2 3 4 5 6 7 8 9 14 13 12 11 10 09

Please note that the lyrics to some of the recordings mentioned in this book may not be suitable for young
audiences.

TABLE OF CONTENTS

Introduction 4

#1 The Beatles 6

#2 Elvis Presley 10

#3 Johnny Cash 14

#4 Ray Charles 18

#5 Aretha Franklin 22

#6 Jimi Hendrix 26

#7 Michael Jackson 30

#8 U2 34

#9 Madonna 38

#10 Run-DMC 42

Honorable Mentions 46

Glossary/For More Information 47

Index 48

Words in the glossary appear in **bold** type
the first time they are used in the text.

THE ULTIMATE **10** Entertainment

Music Legends

Welcome to The Ultimate 10! This exciting series highlights the very best from the world of entertainment.

Grab a front row seat—you're about to meet some of the greatest performers in music history. Some will make you want to twist. Some will make you want to shout. All will make you want to sing along.

U2 performs sold-out concerts all over the world.

This book tells the stories of 10 "ultimate" artists who popularized new forms of music: rock and roll, soul, rhythm and blues (R&B), and hip-hop. Get to know the stars and the stories behind the scenes. Read about the ways music changes how people look, think, and talk. You may never listen to music quite the same way again.

Listen Up!

These 10 pioneering performers changed the world of music.

 #1 The Beatles

 **#2** Elvis Presley

 **#3** Johnny Cash

 **#4** Ray Charles

 **#5** Aretha Franklin

 **#6** Jimi Hendrix

 **#7** Michael Jackson

 #8 U2

 **#9** Madonna

 **#10** Run-DMC

The Beatles
The Fab Four

Rock and roll started in the United States in the 1950s. Rock's early superstars were all American. Then, in 1964, a British rock band called the Beatles took America by storm. Fans went wild. The Beatles paved the way for other British bands, including the Rolling Stones. They also changed the rules of rock and roll. In the process, they influenced every popular musician to this day.

FAST FACTS

Band Members: John Lennon, Paul McCartney, George Harrison, Ringo Starr

First Album: *Please Please Me* (1963)

Ultimate Album: *Sgt. Pepper's Lonely Hearts Club Band* (1967)

The Beatles appear on *The Ed Sullivan Show* in 1964. This made them huge stars in the United States.

Taking the World by Storm

The four Beatles—John Lennon, Paul McCartney, George Harrison, and Ringo Starr—first played together in the summer of 1962. That fall, the Beatles released their first single, "Love Me Do."

The Beatles conquered the world in 1964. They made several historic appearances on *The Ed Sullivan Show* in New York. They also filmed their first movie, *A Hard Day's Night*. At one point that year, they had the top five hit songs on the charts. It remains the only time in rock history that this has happened.

Fans loved the way the Beatles looked—especially their long, "moptop" haircuts. Audiences also loved the way the Beatles acted. Wherever the band members went, they were mobbed by screaming, crying teenagers. This was called Beatlemania.

> **"The Beatles were so big that it's hard for people not alive at the time to realize just how big they were."**
> —Mick Jagger of the Rolling Stones

Music Men

Each member of the Beatles had great talent and creativity. Their music quickly went from simple, fun "yeah-yeah-yeah" songs like "She Loves You" to more complex and original music. The Beatles tried something different with each new album, and each time it worked. Every album became a classic. In 1966, at the peak of their fame, the Beatles stopped touring to focus on recording. Still, they remained wildly successful. Many music **critics** and fans consider *Sgt. Pepper's Lonely Hearts Club Band* to be the greatest album of all time.

The Beatles pose in 1967. They are (left to right): Paul McCartney, Ringo Starr, John Lennon, and George Harrison.

FOR THE RECORD

It takes a great song by a great performer to make it to the top of the charts. Here are the artists with the most number-one hits:

The Beatles   20 #1 hits
First #1 hit: "I Want to Hold Your Hand" (1964)
Most recent #1 hit: "The Long and Winding Road" (1970)

Mariah Carey   18 #1 hits
First #1 hit: "Vision of Love" (1990)
Most recent #1 hit: "Touch My Body" (2006)

Elvis Presley   17 #1 hits
First #1 hit: "Heartbreak Hotel" (1956)
Most recent #1 hit: "Suspicious Minds" (1969)

Michael Jackson   13 #1 hits
First #1 hit: "Ben" (1972)
Most recent #1 hit: "You Are Not Alone" (1995)

Source: Billboard

Paul McCartney is one of the most successful songwriters of all time.

John Lennon's death shocked people around the world. His fans gathered to mourn him and celebrate his life.

The Breakup

The Beatles made more great albums, including *Abbey Road* and *Let It Be*. The band members wanted to move in different directions musically. In 1970, the band split up. Each of the Beatles started a successful solo career. Fans always hoped that they would reunite. A couple of times, they came close. Then, in 1980, Lennon was murdered. His death ended any possibility of a reunion.

The Beatles remain very influential—and popular. In 2000, an album called *1* was released. It includes every Beatles song that reached number one on either the British or the American pop chart. By 2009, the album had sold more than 30 million copies around the world. It was the best-selling album of the decade.

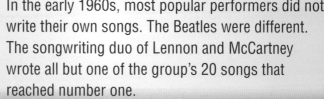

DID YOU KNOW?

In the early 1960s, most popular performers did not write their own songs. The Beatles were different. The songwriting duo of Lennon and McCartney wrote all but one of the group's 20 songs that reached number one.

#2

Elvis Presley
The King

Some music fans say that history can be divided into two periods: B.E. (Before Elvis) and A.E. (After Elvis). They're exaggerating, of course, but the claim has an element of truth. No other entertainer changed the way people look, act, think, and dress the way Elvis Presley did. And no one had a bigger effect on rock and roll. That's why he's called the King of Rock and Roll.

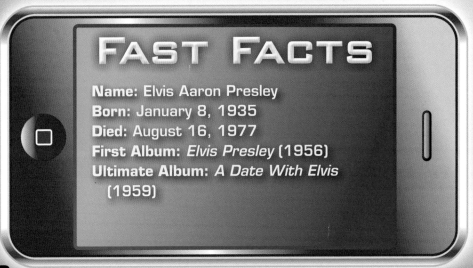

FAST FACTS

Name: Elvis Aaron Presley
Born: January 8, 1935
Died: August 16, 1977
First Album: *Elvis Presley* (1956)
Ultimate Album: *A Date With Elvis*
   (1959)

Elvis Presley's hip-swaying dance moves were seen as shocking in the 1950s. But today they would seem tame.

Teen Sensation

> **"There is only one king."**
> —Bruce Springsteen, on Elvis

Sam Phillips of Sun Records in Memphis, Tennessee, had his finger on the pulse of popular music in 1954. Young people listened to fun-loving **honky-tonk** tunes. They also liked **rhythm and blues (R&B)** performed by African American artists. Phillips knew that the next big star would be a white singer who sang like a black R&B singer.

Then Phillips heard 19-year-old Elvis Presley sing "That's All Right Mama." Phillips knew he'd found what he was after. The handsome singer would become the king of **rockabilly**. Rockabilly was a hard-driving, energetic form of music that mixed R&B and country.

Superstar

By 1956, Presley was selling so many records that Sun couldn't make them fast enough. Presley signed a **recording contract** with RCA, a powerful company in the entertainment business. Songs such as "Heartbreak Hotel" and "Jailhouse Rock" became some of the first great rock and roll songs. Presley was a sensation. Kids loved his raw energy. Parents were afraid of him.

Four future music legends record at Sun Records in the 1950s. They are (left to right): Jerry Lee Lewis, Carl Perkins, Elvis Presley, and Johnny Cash.

FOR THE RECORD

At the time of his death, Elvis held almost every major record in rock and roll:

- More than **700 songs recorded**
- More than **600 million records sold**
- **45 songs** that sold a million copies
- More than **1,000 major concerts** performed
  … and **100 Cadillacs owned!**

In the 1970s, Presley had great success as a live act. During this time, he often wore glittering white suits on stage.

Rising and Falling

Presley's first movie, *Love Me Tender*, was released when he was 21 years old. He would eventually make more than 30 movies. Presley was making so many records and movies that he seldom performed live. Then, in 1968, he made a comeback with a live TV special. He sounded like the Elvis of old! In the 1970s, Presley went back on the road and reconnected with his old fans.

As Presley entered his 40s, his health suffered. In 1977, at age 42, he had a heart attack and died. Presley is buried at Graceland, his beloved home in Memphis. But for millions of fans, the King will live forever through his music.

DID YOU KNOW?

In 1973, Presley gave a concert in Hawaii. It was the first show beamed by satellite around the world. More than 1 billion people saw him perform.

Johnny Cash
The Man in Black

In the mid-1950s, country music and rock and roll were new art forms. Johnny Cash was at the center of both. Over the years, country and rock developed different sounds and different fans. Cash's hard-driving songs and deep voice appealed to fans of both. He walked the line between the two forms of music for much of his career. Today, "country rock" is a category itself thanks to the Man in Black.

FAST FACTS

Name: J. R. "Johnny" Cash
Born: February 26, 1932
Died: September 12, 2003
First Album: *Johnny Cash With His Hot and Blue Guitar* (1957)
Ultimate Album: *Johnny Cash at San Quentin* (1969)

Rural Roots

Johnny Cash's mother taught him how to play guitar. He grew up listening to gospel music and playing gospel tunes on the guitar. Cash's family struggled to make ends meet. He and his older brother, Jack, worked hard alongside their parents to help out. When Johnny was 12, Jack died in an accident. Johnny never got over the loss. Throughout his life, Cash's songs had a deep sadness.

In 1955, Cash auditioned for Sam Phillips of Sun Records. Phillips had discovered Elvis Presley. Phillips liked Cash's deep voice and hard guitar strumming. It was just the sound rockabilly fans wanted to hear. A year later, "I Walk the Line" became Cash's first big hit.

"Until things are brighter, I'm the Man in Black."
—Johnny Cash

Johnny Cash was called the Man in Black because he always wore black on stage. At the time, many country performers wore flashy cowboy outfits.

Reese Witherspoon and Joaquin Phoenix star as June Carter and Johnny Cash in the 2005 film *Walk the Line.*

The Outlaw

During the 1960s, Cash became known as the outlaw of country music. He pushed country music in new directions. One of Cash's biggest hits was "Ring of Fire." It was cowritten by singer June Carter. Cash was in love with Carter, but for many years she refused to marry him. Finally, in 1968, Carter said yes. The couple lived and worked together for the next 35 years.

FOR THE RECORD

One of Johnny Cash's most famous songs is "Folsom Prison Blues." The song is told from the point of view of a prisoner in jail for murder, yearning for freedom. In the late 1960s, Cash performed a series of legendary concerts inside prisons. These performances produced two hit albums, *Johnny Cash at Folsom Prison* and *Johnny Cash at San Quentin.* Cash's popularity among prisoners contributed to his outlaw image.

Cash performs for inmates at Folsom Prison in 1968.

The Man and His Music

Cash inspired many other talented singers and songwriters, in many **genres** of music. He used his fame to defend country music "outsiders." Cash believed that country music should embrace new ideas. During the 1990s, Cash became a favorite of many rock fans. He sang with the rock band U2 on their song "The Wanderer."

In 1994, Cash released *American Recordings*. On this album, he performed songs by several current artists. The album features only his voice and an **acoustic** guitar. A whole new generation of fans discovered what made him great. Using only his voice, Cash could make any song his own.

Johnny Cash's long, black coat and black guitar were auctioned off in 2004, a year after his death.

DID YOU KNOW?

Cash's parents named their son J. R. because they could not agree on a name. He changed it to John R. when he joined the Air Force. He then changed it to Johnny when he signed his first record deal.

Ray Charles
The Birth of Soul

For Ray Charles, it was always about the music. He went to a school for the blind and learned to play many musical instruments. He performed in many bands as a young man, learning different music styles. Charles could do it all. Other musicians called him a genius. In the end, he combined country, blues, gospel, and jazz into a new form of music: soul.

FAST FACTS

Name: Ray Charles Robinson
Born: September 23, 1930
Died: June 10, 2004
First Album: *Ray Charles* (1957)
Ultimate Album: *The Very Best of Ray Charles* (2000)

Ray Charles thrilled audiences with his rhythmic, energetic piano playing.

Staying Power

What does it take to stay at the top of the charts for 50 years? Ray Charles knew the answer to that question. He recorded major hits in almost every type of music. He sang blues for older African American audiences. He sang rock and R&B for younger ones. Many fans liked his songs that blended gospel music with jazz. Later, he recorded several country music hits.

Charles had gone blind at age seven. He soon began attending a school for the blind. There, his musical talent developed.

"I was born with music inside me. Music was one of my parts. Like my ribs, my kidneys, my liver, my heart. Like my blood."
—Ray Charles

Mix Master

Ray Charles spent many years during the 1940s and 1950s trying to become a star. He had some small hits. Then, he really broke through in 1959 with "What'd I Say." The song was a mix of gospel, blues, and rock music. It was his first million-seller. Over the next few years, Charles had number-one hits on the pop chart ("Georgia on My Mind"), R&B chart ("Unchain My Heart"), and country chart ("I Can't Stop Loving You").

Charles performed with back-up singers called the Raelettes. Their powerful, feisty vocals were at the heart of such hits as "Hit the Road Jack" and "The Right Time."

The Raelettes began performing with Ray Charles in the late 1950s. More than a dozen different women were Raelettes through the years.

FOR THE RECORD

Ray Charles's talent for performing different styles of music made him an excellent **duet** partner. His last album, *Genius Loves Company*, was released after his death in 2004. It won eight **Grammy Awards**. On this album, he sang with stars such as Elton John, Norah Jones (right), Gladys Knight, Van Morrison, and Willie Nelson.

Lasting Impact

Ray Charles's raspy, emotional singing style influenced many artists, both white and black, during the 1960s and 1970s. With his unique style, Charles could make any song his own. He made a memorable version of "America the Beautiful." His version of "Georgia on My Mind" became Georgia's official state song in 1979.

In 1986, Charles was among the first group of musicians voted into the Rock and Roll Hall of Fame. That was hardly a surprise. No other popular musician had success with as many types of music. No other performer influenced as many musicians with such talent and creativity.

> "Soul music is when you take a song and make it a part of yourself—a part that is so real and so true that people think it's really happened to you."
> —Ray Charles

DID YOU KNOW?

The film *Ray*, about Ray Charles's life, was released in 2004. Jamie Foxx (above) won an **Academy Award** in the lead role. Before Foxx was cast, Ray played the piano with him and gave his approval.

#5

Aretha Franklin
Lady Soul

Aretha Franklin is known as the Queen of Soul. Soul music was pure energy and emotion when Franklin arrived. She added the power of gospel and the creativity of jazz. She added the passion of R&B and the fun of pop. She changed soul music forever. Off the stage, Franklin was shy and quiet. The moment the music started, however, she was a force of nature.

FAST FACTS

Name: Aretha Franklin
Born: March 25, 1942
First Album: *The Gospel Sound of Aretha Franklin* (1956)
Ultimate Album: *The Very Best of Aretha Franklin: The 60's* (1994)

Choir Girl

Like many great soul artists, Aretha Franklin grew up singing in a church choir. Her father, C. L. Franklin, was a Baptist preacher. His church in Detroit attracted the top religious singers. Franklin's first teachers included gospel legends Mahalia Jackson and Clara Ward.

Franklin performed on the gospel circuit with them and with other stars, including pop music superstar Sam Cooke. He convinced her to try mainstream music. After several years with Columbia Records, Franklin signed with Atlantic Records in 1966. At Atlantic, she reshaped soul music with songs such as "Respect."

> **"If you have the ability to feel, and the ability to hear, then you know that Aretha is still a gospel singer."**
> —C. L. Franklin, Aretha's father

Aretha Franklin began her career as a gospel singer. With her powerful voice, she soon crossed over into pop music.

Aretha Franklin has won many awards for her music.

Royal Success

From 1967 to 1973, Aretha Franklin was the reigning Queen of Soul. She was backed by the incredible Muscle Shoals Rhythm Section. Their music matched the power of Aretha's voice. Franklin could turn any song into solid gold. She **arranged** many of them herself.

Franklin loved to mix the "call-and-response" gospel style into her songs. She would sing a word or two. Other singers would then respond by singing the same word. Often the "response" voices belonged to her sisters, Erma and Carolyn.

FOR THE RECORD

Over an amazing eight-year period, Aretha Franklin scored 13 number-one hits on the R&B chart.

YEAR	SONG
1967	"I Never Loved a Man"
	"Respect"
	"Baby I Love You"
1968	"Chain of Fools"
	"Since You've Been Gone"
	"Think"
1969	"Share Your Love With Me"
1970	"Call Me"
	"Don't Play That Song"
1971	"Bridge Over Troubled Water"
	"Spanish Harlem"
1972	"Day Dreaming"
1973	"Until You Come Back to Me"

Mariah Carey and Aretha Franklin perform on VH1's *Divas Live*.

Soul Inspiration

During the 1960s and 1970s, Aretha Franklin became a powerful symbol of African American pride. She was active in the civil rights movement. She appeared with Martin Luther King Jr. many times before his death in 1968.

In 1987, Franklin was the first woman voted into the Rock and Roll Hall of Fame. Three years later, she released her 50th album. In 2008, *Rolling Stone* magazine named her the number-one singer of all time. The many powerful singers she inspired—from Whitney Houston to Mariah Carey to Beyoncé Knowles—would definitely agree!

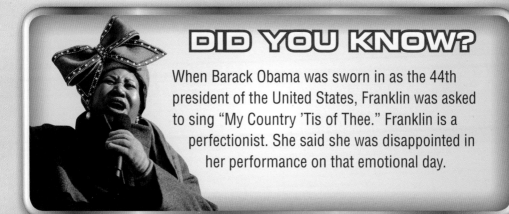

DID YOU KNOW?

When Barack Obama was sworn in as the 44th president of the United States, Franklin was asked to sing "My Country 'Tis of Thee." Franklin is a perfectionist. She said she was disappointed in her performance on that emotional day.

Jimi Hendrix
Three Years of Fire

Guitars have always been at the center of rock and roll. When Jimi Hendrix arrived on the scene in the mid-1960s, he changed how musicians viewed guitars. In his hands, the guitar came alive. It made sounds that had never been heard before. Hendrix had just gotten started when his career was cut short. Fans still wonder where he might have taken music had he lived longer.

FAST FACTS

Name: Jimi Hendrix
Born: November 27, 1942
Died: September 18, 1970
First Album: *Are You Experienced* (1967)
Ultimate Album: *The Jimi Hendrix Concerts* (1981)

Jimi Hendrix was left-handed, but he did not play a left-handed guitar. Instead, he played a right-handed guitar upside down.

Paying His Dues

Jimi Hendrix was born to a Cherokee mother and an African American father. His mother died when he was a teenager. His father bought him a guitar and taught him how to play jazz and blues. Hendrix spent hours alone, mastering the guitar. Then he made it do things no one else could.

Hendrix was an amazing musician. He was more than just talented. In the early 1960s, Hendrix worked as "Jimmy James" with such legendary soul and blues performers as Ike and Tina Turner, B. B. King, Sam Cooke, Jackie Wilson, and Little Richard.

"When I get up on stage, well, that's my whole life. That's my religion."
—Jimi Hendrix

London Calling

In 1965, Chas Chandler of the rock band the Animals brought Hendrix to London, England. He introduced him to bass player Noel Redding and drummer Mitch Mitchell. Together, they formed the Jimi Hendrix Experience. Their single "Purple Haze" and album *Are You Experienced* made the band the hit of London's rock scene.

In 1967, Hendrix returned to the United States. He performed at the Monterey Pop Festival. There, he gave a jaw-dropping performance. His playing and singing were miles ahead of the other bands at the festival. When he was done, Hendrix set his guitar on fire!

Jimi Hendrix plays at the Woodstock music festival.

FOR THE RECORD

Hendrix played the longest set of his career at the Woodstock music festival in 1969. He was on stage for two hours. Hendrix's long, loud, defiant version of "The Star-Spangled Banner" is one of the great symbols of the 1960s.

Guitar Man

For the next three years, Hendrix was all serious rock fans wanted to talk about. People bought his albums and flocked to his concerts. Other guitarists pushed themselves to keep up with his raw, explosive talent. Meanwhile, Hendrix pushed himself to even greater heights. He built a studio in New York where he could experiment with new sounds.

By the summer of 1970, Hendrix was exhausted. He had blazed across the music scene for three years and needed to rest. Unfortunately, Hendrix had trouble sleeping. One night, he took too many sleeping pills and died. But his influence—and his legend—live on.

During concerts, Jimi Hendrix sometimes played his guitar with his teeth. He also played behind his back!

DID YOU KNOW?

In 2003, *Rolling Stone* magazine named Jimi Hendrix the greatest guitarist of all time.

#7

Michael Jackson
The King of Pop

Some say that being a rock star means you never have to grow up. That suited Michael Jackson just fine. He had been a music superstar since he was 11 years old. He was shy in real life but electrifying on stage. Every note, every move, every moment was magical. Jackson brought tremendous joy and energy to his songs. And during the 1980s, no one was bigger or better than the King of Pop was.

FAST FACTS

Name: Michael Jackson
Born: August 29, 1958
Died: June 25, 2009
First Album: *Got to Be There* (1971)
Ultimate Album: *Thriller* (1982)

A Young Superstar

Before Michael Jackson became a solo superstar, he and his brothers were part of the Jackson 5. They were one of the most successful family groups ever.

Michael was the lead singer for the Jackson 5. He helped the group score major hits with "ABC," "I'll Be There," and "Never Can Say Goodbye." They were a huge success, but the brothers worked constantly. It was exhausting. When Michael was 12, he began recording solo albums.

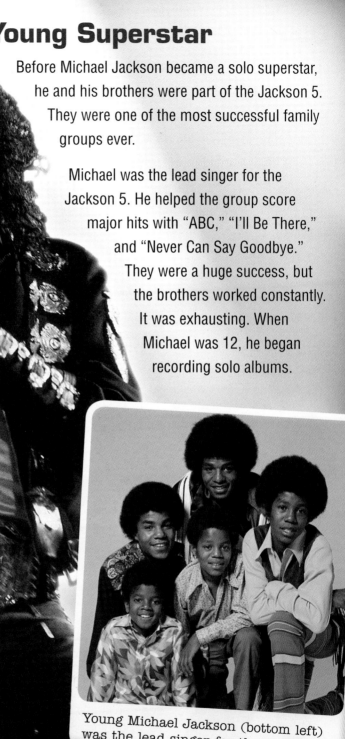

Young Michael Jackson (bottom left) was the lead singer for the Jackson 5.

Quincy & Me

In 1978, Jackson played the Scarecrow in *The Wiz*, a modern version of *The Wizard of Oz*. He met record **producer** Quincy Jones while making the film. In 1979, they teamed up to release *Off The Wall*. The songs appealed to everyone, young and old. People who liked rock, funk, and disco all liked the album. It made Jackson a solo superstar.

In late 1982, Jackson released *Thriller*. The album was the number-one seller in the United States for 37 weeks. Jackson got to show off his amazing dance moves in the *Thriller* videos. People could not take their eyes off him.

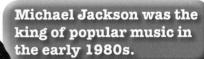

Michael Jackson was the king of popular music in the early 1980s.

FOR THE RECORD

When MTV first began broadcasting in 1981, most videos simply showed a band playing a song. Then, in 1982, Michael Jackson's album *Thriller* was released. Videos for "Beat It," "Billie Jean," and other songs on *Thriller* were not simple and straightforward. They had intense story lines and large dance numbers. They were art. Many people tuned into MTV just to see Jackson's videos, and the channel became very popular.

Ola Ray and Jackson perform in the "Thriller" video.

Man of the World

Jackson used his fame to help others. He was deeply concerned with worldwide poverty. In 1985, he and singer Lionel Ritchie wrote "We Are the World." They gathered the top names in music to film a video. Sales of the video and song generated millions of dollars for needy people worldwide.

Justin Timberlake (left) performs with Jackson at a special concert in 2001.

During the 1990s, Jackson continued to create new music. He gave millions of dollars away to help people in need. Since then, he influenced a new generation of pop stars, from Usher to Beyoncé Knowles to Justin Timberlake. Jackson, who was preparing for a comeback tour, died unexpectedly on June 25, 2009, at the age of 50.

"Michael Jackson has made a bigger impact on music than any other artist in the history of music. He was magic. ... He will always be the King of Pop!"

—R&B singer Beyoncé Knowles

DID YOU KNOW?

Michael Jackson's greatest dance moment came during the TV special *25 Years of Motown* in 1983. He performed his hit song "Billie Jean" and thrilled millions by unveiling the moonwalk. This dance move made it look like he was walking forward while he was actually moving backward.

U2

Staying on Top

In 1985, *Rolling Stone* magazine called the Irish band U2 the "band of the 80s." Many fans would say that U2 was the band of the 1990s and of this decade, too. The band has stayed on top by mixing high energy, soaring guitars, and the larger-than-life voice of lead singer Bono. Also, U2 uses its music to focus attention on social injustices and human rights causes.

FAST FACTS

Band Members: Paul "Bono" Hewson, Dave "The Edge" Evans, Adam Clayton, Larry Mullen Jr.
First Album: *Boy* (1980)
Ultimate Album: *The Joshua Tree* (1987)

The Edge (left) and Bono of the band U2 perform in Switzerland in 2005.

Good From the Get-Go

Fast starts are unusual in the music business. Normally, a band's first album is a way to introduce its sound to a wide audience. When U2 released *Boy* in 1980, no one could remember a more powerful **debut album**. The band's music wasn't typical punk or rock. It had a sound all its own.

The group had started playing together as teens in the 1970s. Each member was creative, but they were not expert musicians. This led to U2's early style. It featured simple, pounding rhythms and heavy guitar chords.

"I want people to leave our concerts feeling positive, a little more free."
—Bono

Music and Meaning

U2 became a worldwide sensation in 1987 with *The Joshua Tree*. The group's music and message won it many awards that year. The group went on a sold-out worldwide concert tour. In 1988, U2 released another hit album, *Rattle and Hum*. U2 became known as the band with a conscience. The band members used their fame to help fight hunger, racism, and poverty.

The band members are (left to right): The Edge, Adam Clayton, Bono, and Larry Mullen Jr.

FOR THE RECORD

Through the years, U2 has been amazingly productive and won many awards:

- In 2005, U2 won five Grammy Awards—the most ever won by a band in a single night.
- By 2009, U2 had won 22 Grammy Awards—more than any other band.
- As of 2009, U2 had sold nearly 150 million albums worldwide.

Bono meets children in a village in Tanzania. His efforts to end poverty have taken him all around the world.

Changing the Game

In 1991, U2 surprised fans with *Achtung Baby*. The album had a totally different style, with funkier beats and sad love songs. During the 1990s, U2 put on bigger and bigger concerts and experimented even more with their music.

U2's sound changed again in the first years of the 21st century. With *All That You Can't Leave Behind* in 2000, U2 started an era of smart, soulful rock and roll that continues to this day.

DID YOU KNOW?

Bono has used his fame to help people around the world. He has worked to provide food and medicine to help the needy in poor countries. He has met world leaders such as U.S. president Bill Clinton and the late Pope John Paul II, urging them to help.

#9

Madonna
The Material Girl

How do you become a pop music star? Talent alone is not enough. You also have to be smart and sensational. No singer has been smarter or more sensational than Madonna. She has stayed at the top of the business for a quarter century. During that time, she has constantly changed her look and her sound. In doing so, the Material Girl changed popular culture.

FAST FACTS

Name: Madonna Louise Ciccone
Born: August 16, 1958
First Album: *Madonna* (1983)
Ultimate Album: *The Immaculate Collection* (1990)

Madonna performs at a concert in 1985. At the time, she was known for her wild clothes and energetic performances.

Video Superstar

In the early days of music videos, the music channel MTV was looking for a superstar. It found one in Madonna. She had a street-smart attitude and a wild wardrobe. Her songs were funky and catchy and easy to dance to. Madonna's playful videos turned her into a star almost overnight.

"Even when I was a little girl, I knew I wanted the whole world to know who I was, to love me and be affected by me."
—Madonna

What Madonna did next made her a music legend. With each new video, she changed her look. Madonna didn't do this to follow pop fashion. She did it to *lead* pop fashion. By the end of the 1980s, she was one of the most famous entertainers on the planet.

Full of Surprises

Whenever Madonna's fans thought she had run out of new ideas or surprises, she did something incredible. She has never been afraid to shock people with her songs and videos. In 1990, she helped spark a dance craze with the song "Vogue." Later, Madonna was one of the first rock stars to raise money for research to fight the deadly disease AIDS.

Madonna's video for "Like a Prayer" caused a lot of controversy.

FOR THE RECORD

Madonna has appeared in more than 20 movies. These are some of her most famous starring roles:

YEAR	ROLE
1985	Susan in *Desperately Seeking Susan*
1986	Gloria in *Shanghai Surprise*
1987	Nikki in *Who's That Girl?*
1990	Breathless Mahoney in *Dick Tracy*
1992	Mae Mordabito in *A League of Their Own*
1996	Eva Peron in *Evita*

Madonna stars as Eva Peron in *Evita*.

Madonna performs during her sold-out tour in 2008. She is still going strong, even past age 50.

The Hits Keep Coming

In the 1990s, Madonna started Maverick Records. She kept making new dance records. At the same time, she assisted the young musicians she signed. Madonna helped make stars of Alanis Morissette and Michelle Branch. Among the many artists Madonna influenced are Britney Spears and Christina Aguilera.

Just when Madonna's fans thought she might finally be settling down, she surprised them again. In 2008, she went on a worldwide concert tour. The tour made more money than any tour by a solo artist in history. That same year, Madonna was voted into the Rock and Roll Hall of Fame.

DID YOU KNOW?

In 2005, Madonna's career took a surprising turn when she published her first children's book, *The English Roses*. She has since written more than a dozen other children's books.

#10

Run-DMC
Hip-Hop Goes Big

When Elvis Presley got his start, many people thought rock and roll was a fad. In the 1980s, some people said the same thing about hip-hop and rap. Run-DMC made sure that hip-hop was here to stay. They did so by giving their music a harder beat and an in-your-face attitude. Suddenly, everyone was listening, from the suburbs to the city streets.

FAST FACTS

Band Members: Joey "Run" Simmons, Darryl "DMC" McDaniels, Jason "Jam-Master Jay" Mizell
First Album: *Run-D.M.C.* (1983)
Ultimate Album: *Raising Hell* (1986)

Queens Connection

The three young men who joined forces to become Run-DMC grew up in the Hollis neighborhood of Queens, New York. Joey Simmons was the younger brother of Russell Simmons, a hip-hop promoter. Through Russell, Joey began working as a DJ for superstar Kurtis Blow. Audiences loved when he beat-boxed, making percussion sounds with his mouth. Simmons and his friend Darryl McDaniels worked on their rap lyrics together.

In 1980, they decided to try out their rhymes on a popular DJ named Jason Mizell. The three became fast friends and started working together. In 1983, Russell Simmons agreed to help them get a recording contract.

"The whole purpose of hip-hop is to inspire, to motivate and to educate."

—Darryl "DMC" McDaniels

The members of Run-DMC got their start in New York City. They are (left to right): Joey Simmons, Darryl McDaniels, and Jason Mizell.

Rocking Out

In the early days of rap, groups focused on making singles for dance clubs. Run-DMC turned the focus to making albums. Their first album came in 1984. It had a song called "Rock Box." This song blended hard rock with hip-hop in a way no one had tried before. The group also created a new look. They wore Adidas shoes and thick gold chains. Almost overnight, hip-hop fashion changed.

On Run-DMC's third album, the band Aerosmith performed their classic hit "Walk This Way." In the video, the two groups break down a wall between a rock performance and a rap performance. The song did the same thing for the music industry.

The members of Run-DMC were pioneers of modern hip-hop fashion.

FOR THE RECORD

Russell Simmons, Joey Simmons's older brother, is one of the most successful people in the music industry. He co-founded Def Jam Records. The record label signed top hip-hop performers such as Public Enemy, LL Cool J, and the Beastie Boys. Simmons also founded the Phat Farm clothing line.

Russell Simmons (right) poses with hip-hop artist Jay-Z.

Darryl "DMC" McDaniels performs with Kid Rock (left) and Steven Tyler of Aerosmith (center).

Changing Times

During the 1990s, Run-DMC experimented with new sounds. Simmons and McDaniels sometimes disagreed on what the group should do next. In 2001, the men put their differences aside and went on a successful concert tour. Run-DMC fans were sure that the group was ready to do more great things. Then, in 2002, Mizell was shot and killed outside his recording studio. The murder was never solved. Run-DMC never recorded again.

Run-DMC changed hip-hop music and expanded hip-hop's audience. In 2007, MTV named Run-DMC the greatest hip-hop group of all time. Two years later, in 2009, the group became only the second hip-hop group to be voted into the Rock and Roll Hall of Fame.

DID YOU KNOW?

At the age of 35, Darryl McDaniels found out that he was adopted. His search for his biological parents was the subject of the 2006 film *DMC: My Adoption Journey*.

Bob Dylan

Born: May 24, 1941

Ultimate Album: *Highway 61 Revisited* (1965)

For Bob Dylan, a great song starts with the lyrics. He was rock's first poet. Dylan has set his words to almost any style of music, from folk to rock to country to **reggae**. His lyrics have influenced countless songwriters over the past 40 years.

The Rolling Stones

Band Members: Mick Jagger, Keith Richards, Charlie Watts, Ron Wood, Bill Wyman

Ultimate Album: *Beggar's Banquet* (1968)

The long-lived English rock band the Rolling Stones based their music on the blues. They first brought their sound to the United States during the 1960s **British Invasion** and have been going strong ever since. The group's brash, hard-driving hits include "Jumping Jack Flash" and "Start Me Up."

Bob Marley

Born: February 6, 1945   **Died:** May 11, 1981

Ultimate Album: *Legend* (1984)

Bob Marley and the Wailers brought the Afro-Caribbean beat of reggae to the world. Reggae often features strong, relaxed rhythms and lyrics on topics ranging from religion to social justice. Marley's popularity helped draw attention to the struggles of the poor in Jamaica.

Glossary

Academy Award: an award given each year for achievement in movies

acoustic: related to a musical instrument that has a sound that has not been boosted electronically

arranged: decided how the music for a song should sound

British Invasion: a period from 1964 to 1967 when British rock bands first became popular in the United States

critics: people who review music, film, books, and other forms of art

debut album: the first collection of songs created for sale to the public by a band or singer

duet: a musical piece sung or played by two artists

genres: categories of music, such as rock, soul, or country

Grammy Awards: awards given each year for outstanding achievements in the music industry

honky-tonk: upbeat country music from the 1940s and 1950s

producer: someone who is in charge of making a record, film, or TV show

recording contract: an agreement between a singer and a record company in which the singer agrees to make a record and the company agrees to sell it

reggae: a type of music developed in Jamaica that blends many styles, including jazz and rhythm and blues

rhythm and blues (R&B): a smooth musical style that borrows from different forms of African American music, including jazz, gospel, and blues

rockabilly: music that mixes features of rock and country music

For More Information

Books

Bergamini, Andrea. *The History of Rock Music.* Hauppauge, NY: Barron's Educational Books, 2000.

George-Warren, Holly. *Shake, Rattle & Roll: The Founders of Rock & Roll.* New York: Sandpiper Books, 2004.

Kallen, Stuart. *The History of Rock and Roll.* San Diego: Lucent Books, 2002.

Krull, Kathleen. *The Book of Rock Stars.* New York: Hyperion, 2003.

Web Sites

Billboard
www.billboard.com
Find out about today's chart toppers as well as those from past decades.

Rock and Roll Hall of Fame and Museum
www.rockhall.com
Learn about the history of rock and roll on this museum's web site.

Publisher's note to educators and parents: Our editors have carefully reviewed these web sites to ensure that they are suitable for children. Many web sites change frequently, however, and we cannot guarantee that a site's future contents will continue to meet our high standards of quality and educational value. Be advised that children should be closely supervised whenever they access the Internet.

Index

Aerosmith 44

Beatles 6, 7, 8, 9
Blow, Kurtis 43
Bono 34, 35, 37

Carey, Mariah 8, 25
Carter, June 16
Cash, Jack 15
Cash, Johnny 14, 15, 16, 17
Chandler, Chas 28
Charles, Ray 18, 19, 20, 21
Clayton, Adam 34
concerts 12, 13, 16, 28, 29,
   35, 36, 37, 41, 45
Cooke, Sam 23, 27

Def Jam Records 44
Dylan, Bob 46

The Ed Sullivan Show 7
The Edge 34

Franklin, Aretha 22, 23, 24,
   25
Franklin, Carolyn 24
Franklin, C. L. 23
Franklin, Erma 24

Grammy Awards 20, 36

Harrison, George 6, 7

Hendrix, Jimi 26, 27, 28, 29

Jackson 5 31
Jackson, Michael 8, 30, 31,
   32, 33
Jagger, Mick 7, 46
Jimi Hendrix Experience 28
Jones, Norah 20
Jones, Quincy 32

King, Martin Luther, Jr. 25
Knowles, Beyoncé, 33

Lennon, John 6, 7, 9

Madonna 38, 39, 40, 41
Marley, Bob 46
Martin, Ricky 33
Maverick Records 41
McCartney, Paul 6, 7, 9
McDaniels, Darryl "DMC" 42,
   43, 45
Mitchell, Mitch 28
Mizell, Jason "Jam-Master
   Jay" 42, 43, 45
moonwalk (dance move) 33
movies 7, 13, 21, 32, 40, 45
MTV 32, 39, 45
Mullen, Larry, Jr. 34
Muscle Shoals Rhythm
   Section 24

Obama, Barack 25

Phillips, Sam 11, 15
Presley, Elvis 8, 10, 11, 12,
   13, 15, 42

Raelettes 20
Redding, Noel 28
Richards, Keith 46
Ritchie, Lionel 33
Rock and Roll Hall of Fame
   21, 25, 41, 45
Rolling Stone magazine 25,
   29, 34
Rolling Stones 6, 46
Run-DMC 42, 43, 44, 45

Simmons, Joey "Run" 42,
   43, 45
Simmons, Russell 43, 44
Springsteen, Bruce 11
Starr, Ringo 6, 7
Sun Records 11, 12, 15

U2 17, 34, 35, 36, 37

videos 32, 33, 39, 40, 44

Watts, Charlie 46
Wood, Ron 46
Wyman, Bill 46

About the Author

Mark Stewart has written more than 200 nonfiction books for young people. As a boy in New York City, he attended conductor Leonard Bernstein's Young People's Concerts. Joe Raposo, songwriter for Sesame Street, was a family friend. His stepbrother, Mike Stern, played guitar with jazz legend Miles Davis and was a member of the band Blood, Sweat & Tears.